Southern
Messenger
Poets

DAVE SMITH, EDITOR

LATE LEISURE

LATE LEISURE

poems

ELEANOR ROSS TAYLOR

Louisiana State University Press   *Baton Rouge*   1999

Manufactured in the United States of America
First printing
07   06   05   04   03   02   01   00   99   98   5   4   3   2   1

Designer: Michele Myatt Quinn
Typeface: Bembo, Serlio
Typesetter: Coghill Composition
Printer and binder: Edwards Brothers, Inc.

Library of Congress Cataloging-in-Publication Data

Taylor, Eleanor Ross, 1928–
    Late leisure : poems / Eleanor Ross Taylor.
        p.   cm.—(Southern messenger poets)
    ISBN 0-8071-2355-2 (cloth : alk. paper).—ISBN 0-8071-2356-0 (pbk. : alk. paper).
    I. Title. II. Series.
    PS3570.A9285L38   1999
    811'.54—dc21   98-44081
                                                                              CIP

Grateful acknowledgment is made to the editors of the following publications, in which the poems noted first appeared: *Carolina Quarterly:* "The Accidental Prisoner"; *Cape Rock:* "Shaking the Plum Tree"; *Grand Street:* "The Hostage"; *Greensboro Review:* "Retired Pilot Watches Plane"; *Hollins Critic:* "Cloud Cover," "Find Me"; *Kenyon Review:* "Diary Entry, March 24"; *Key West Review:* "Dust"; *New Yorker:* "Daytime Moon," "Kitchen Fable," "Salting the Oatmeal"; *Paris Review:* "Always Reclusive," "On Being Worldly," "A Place Apart"; *Parnassus:* "Cocoon," "Late Leisure"; *Ploughshares:* "Cuts Buttons Off an Old Sweater"; *Seneca Review:* "Long-Dreaded Event Takes Place," "Te Deum"; *Shenandoah:* "A Harem of Hens," "Sitting in the Dark, Morning," "Sparrow Eats Fried Chicken Wing"; *Southern Review:* "Clothes from Three Planets," "The Diary," "Homecoming," "Katydids Sewanee," "The Sky-Watcher"; *Southwest Review:* "Overgrown Path"; *Verse:* "Completing the Pilgrimage"; *Virginia Quarterly Review:* "Converse"; *Yale Review:* "Night Retrieves," "O Lamp."
    "Why Angels Choir" first appeared in the *Antioch Review,* Vol. 56, No. 1 (Winter 1998). Copyright © 1998 by the Antioch Review, Inc. Reprinted by permission of the Editors.
    "Worlds Old and New" was originally printed in the Simon Daro Dawidowicz Poetry Competition Finalists booklet, from Florida International University Libraries.

The paper in this book meets the guidelines for permanence and durability of the Committee on Production Guidelines for Book Longevity of the Council on Library Resources. ⊗

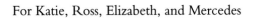

For Katie, Ross, Elizabeth, and Mercedes

CONTENTS

LATE
LEISURE

LONG-DREADED EVENT
TAKES PLACE

it blurs
        happening as on canvas
distanced
       almost out of earshot
           moving unwillingly
in galactic impulse
      not touching me
         crawling   as I
remote, half turned away,
     my eyes half closed
       half watch,

a painter   at my easel
     distancing my sketch
        pretending I recede

not present
     hoping   hoping
       I'm not present
glazed eyes catching
     small smithereens:
       the nurse's ring
bone pink smooth though modified
     the brief convulsive reflex
       and the driver's shoes well tied

everything establishes
     my absence in this scene
       later somewhere
I'll paint-in gaps, fill in
     the larger picture,
       withholdings spilled
out of my pockets of resistance—
     the brushes
       the paints
the skill

DIARY ENTRY, MARCH 24

Today
walked home   tho cold
No coffee   no Crackerjack   no
books $200 cash   3.50 taxi
saved   5.69 coffee not spent
                    Wind blowing
hard   Scarf tossing in my face
breathing fast the cold
A young man   boy   walking
like that boy in Ellerbe   hands deep
in pockets   shoulders twisting
                    mouth bitter
glittering eyes   black-fringed   into looking
Kiss-me-quick-I'm-off-goodbye   tied
my scarf under my chin
                    Hurry
Just past the bridge wind threw
a foam hot dog carton onto
the walk ahead of me   It landed
flat   waddled along open   a little casket
determined to get home first   But
the wind lifted it again   took it off   I,
determined to get there before it
                    Waddle
as the wind blows, casket
                    A fling
of maple keys to street
That's the way the money goes
Keys   eyes bluegray   Black-fringed

Don't shiver little star
It's not as cold as all that

RETIRED PILOT WATCHES PLANE

Through frosted window clearing
    and bifocals   I view as
        through a telescope: 6:00
He's walking Boofy   but stopped
    midstreet looking up
        The early NY flight
slowing for coming in

        He sees?   I can't know   More
        than my party-talk
acquaintance wouldn't help
    His long hand easy on
        the leash   his hairless head
his extra pounds   satanic
    eyes   this guy who wades through
        snow to tuck my paper
at my door   who's sold his plane
    now travels less down to
        his sailboat on the Chesapeake
("Anne doesn't care for it")
    but mentions still   he must:
        sharp spray dark-curling
Boofy's coat   euphoric
    speed   and especially that line
        far out   sea must make
against the sky you try and try
    to see but never find

        His head
turning with the plane   a maze
    of speeds and altitudes?
        controls he is unleashing
there in the cockpit?
        Half dizzy
I come down to

my yard   yews my late
        husband planted   East and color
raying far   no line between
    earth's atmosphere
        black space   no oxygen

He's turned   drifts   Boofy leading
    downstreet to pancakes
        I think, having invented flying
And I think I'll wait a minute
    to get my paper in

Having rebought a fragment of the past
　　I tear my way back through
the path I gardened years ago.
　　Are these the things I planted?
Laurel head-high, snarled with kudzu.
　　You've got it back.
Daffs, in runs, not blooming
　　under ten years' leaves.
Re-do the works.
　　The single multiflora I "might allow"
is upper hand, lassos the foot.
　　Trim canopy for light. No bulbs. Fill in.

　　A dirging crash.
　　Somewhere in umbrage,
　　a dead branch, letting go:

　　　　In here
　　　　is
　　　　1989.
　　　　Somewhere,
　　　　the day
　　　　I scuttled Benedict.
　　　　The afternoon I missed my train
　　　　and went back to their icy eyes.
　　　　The night—

No bulbs. Fill in. Plant-over
all this noxious mess of bramble roots.

SALTING THE OATMEAL

She never used a measuring spoon.
   She poured salt in her palm
      and flung it in the oatmeal.
Some days it rained all day.
   Some winters it never snowed.
      Her second marriage might have worked.
What if she'd used a measuring spoon?
   The bombers flew over every night
      but she never had to be dug out.
Sometimes she reached for the saltcellar.
   When we were in Austria,
      Hans cadged petrol and passports
         from three countries. . . .
            We had to leave Herr Mohl behind.
            And my mauve accordion. . . .
When things were too salty
   she drank a glass of water
      or most anything.

A stubborn foxgray shack.
One bending oak too claybound to fall down.
   Here the schoolbus turned
   and went back to the world.

We watched nine children exit headlong,
   tear off three ways . . .
                their dens.

All, my mother said, in this backwoods
   some kin to me.
   The idiot brother. The crazy uncle, too.
The white-browed figure
   in a black plush
   hat off some Colonial shelf,
there sometimes, stockstill
   as his stick . . .
             some kin.

Two miles back
   we'd left the road,
   gone through a trestle, down
a tunnel fringe-trees and wild bloom,
   huffing at the wheels.
   Bumps and splashes. Birds
unaccustomed scudding off the lane.
   Hounds sleeping around washpots
   black-nosed, sleep-deprived.
The house in which our Civil War
   deserter kin made good his hide.

Sometimes the student driver
   intoned archly: "All out for
   Kimmerville!" for benefit of Kimreys
who never took a book home,
   walked off with every prize.

I liked going through the tunnel twice.
When we re-did the trestle, climbed
    back up to home road, day joined us
    where we'd left it. Rote fences
and home houses flicked by
    like TV frames, not yet invented.

In my Platonic heaven I too get off the bus.
    It rounds the longing tree,
    no danger to the foxgray steps,
then snails back toward warm
    quilts and milk, is gone

I break and run for Kimmerville.

KATYDIDS SEWANEE

Some night this rasping of green wings
will metamorphose
to propellers   pluck
this village off the mountain
    peeling
        peeling
            topsoil
                rhododendrons
                    from ravines
lift
    the slowly waking deer
        and echo fawn
            peeling
                pulling
                    plucking up
the willing chapel
    windows flashing
        tumbling moonlight
            peeling
                softly
                    with a lyric grace
the graveyard   raising rain-gnawed markers
"Miss Charlotte Elliott"   and
"John Orley Allen
Tate" with these loud wings
    invisible but
        green
            clapping
                a distant
                clapping
as in
an auditorium closed
to one out in the vestibule
    the whole
        Domain
            on wing

over the breathstealing valley
over twanging Nashville
the reddened
    Mississippi
       over long exoduses
         crawling
           vaporous warriors
Sewanee night
deployed
wing- by wingload
   around the stars
      drummed into
         heaven first without
           form and void

HIS VISIT

Why am I going?

What will she say?
Will she say hello?
Will she say *hello*?
Will she say, Hello?
She'll open the door.
I'll cross the driveway.
I'll knock.
Will she say, Come in?
There are steps, of course.
It's dark.
Will she say, Come in?

She'll come to the door.

Te Deum

Lord

    sho been good to me

       My loved hoe handle, and my sweat,
heart pounding and the towhee singing.

    Jill, jerking the hospital sheets,
       "Damn careless nurses . . .
"But golly . . . a good life.
    "That student who kept writing me.
       "That rainy picnic by a road in Burgundy.
"Heart thumping, thumping on . . . more, more. . . ."

       A squirrel on a post.
The nutgrooved skull
    drops; he claws the dirt.
       Next winter!
Frost thrown down,
    a stiffened morning,
       a harsh corrective herb
to gnaw, take in.

    Sho been, Lord, sho been

       Whether born of kiss sublime,
victim's terror, rapist crime, and
    however ending,
       nut-gnawers nulled
inscrutably, or
    Caesars,
       soldiers, friends
lammed open-eyed—

    Lord, good . . . sho been

A PLACE APART

Hung, awfully, over the valley
    on this remote escarpment,
a long, unearthly house
    of earth-pink stone,
a sanctum made, an alleluia
    on a rock—the bishop's.

Not a sour monk escaped domestic chains:
    daughters and granddaughters
on the plain storybook swing
    have dangled and disappeared.

Much of God's work—the stinted trees
    and laurels grateful for a cleft.
Much of his wife's—the well-staked
    vortexed lilies that obsess
the hummingbird; potted hydrangeas
    and a rare old door.

Inside, a sylvan mural,
    silver urns, a multipartite service;
Louis chairs in this—
    it cries out, gallery;
slim satin sofas stressing
    glassed, gouached views.

But first, his poet guest's
    hard put to find his refuge
in vined folds, descents,
    and passes hemlock hung
behind clerestory oaks
    and a world-fending wall.

The bookroom in this bastion
    opens west on flocks of

gathering mountains.
    Book spines soliloquize, they
beckon explorations with no map
    except his musing
Azalea arborescens trail
    flicked with goldfinches'
twitter and a sheaf of goldenrod,
    the thin leaves of a testament.

He quotes St. Augustine, talks
    fervently of *Father Sergius*,
is frankly pleased with his stone
    railings (that convent at Amalfi
where bees stole back
    their honey from the *pane fritta*),
his aged brick promenades
    leading to beeches on the bluff—
the Cherokees' sacred groves, still,
    it seems, wringing their hands.

If a night storm drags the valley,
    crawls up and breaks,
the angel of the storm
    loud-swishing in the trees,
he flicks the floodlights on
    iron vines of rainlashed chairs,
the roaming lightning
    and the vast, conclusive dark
wholly manifest, scourging
    his balconied Te Deum.

A fragile man,
   whitehaired and insubstantial,
a handful of evolving sparks
   in a dark room, breakfasting
with existing dark after dreams
   riddled and lanced with glory:
Do thou worship in a place apart,
   go shut the door.
And when you give alms, be it in secret.

What is he, whose polished worldly
   unaccountable Eden's proffered Heaven?
The poet, home, pounds
   his soft, common bed,
and unwords poems.

THE NATURE OF GODS

Back home.
     Nobody knows him, but—his land.
They whisper . . . the first Tighe . . . some bigwig.
     His dad made a pile, went to the Pen.
No kin left here. The last one went to
     Spain? Sokane?

     And he, he's been
out to some foreign place where
     starved folks fed their *gods*; then
back in good old USA, to Hollywood,
     signed photos for some star,
answered her fans.

     They slow down,
passing his windows, sashes banged-to Sundays. . . .
     Come Ye Sinners could osmose?
They climb his steps, slip in, and take a chair.
     His traveled face, his odd arrangements
of stray fragments, his touch of elemental squalor,
     that room he takes you into, urns and jars.

     Somebody brings
a window fan. This vile May heat—he's not used to?
     Somebody else, one tuberose.
"There were only three."

     Drugged
by his silence they bleed words.
     —hoped, I always hoped   *It weighed on me*
Nobody got it straight   *We called it off*

     Then
steer their Volvos down his wretched drive
     slowly, through strangely late,
not looking back where he's transfixed
     inventing a rare gate.

THE LIGHTHOUSE KEEPER

The car lights wake me
   in the dark at five,
   the long beams in the next drive
cruising my hinterland,
the safe slip of my single bed.
   It is the lighthouse keeper I half
   dream, bringing the beams
home with her for the day,
into her mama's kitchen
   or garage with her old skis.
                     Some day
snipping at the sink
   she'll hack them short
   and spike them in a vase
for her window. They'll blink.
Beware, missing husband, dropout
   kids, pro tem moonlight job.

DUST

Now that I've put
  my glasses on
  I see
  the goblets I take down
  are furred with dust.
How'd all those years
  skip me?
Can I
  still in
  a dustless time ago,
  in a fool's dustless now,
  be clock-stopped
  by these my goblets
  sotted with dust,
  dust kicked up from old rugs,
  dust of my daily tread
  sieved onto
  these-my-goblets,
  flatting their flash,
  ashing the Médoc's red,
  ashing my lips
  and the goblets' lips,
  daunting the centerpiece,
  wobbling my sight,
  blurring the place cards—
Who's this
  I have invited?

A CHANGE OF STATE

Was it a car?
   A tree limb raked the house?
A lost wasp
   battling bedroom ceiling?
Just time to wake up?

   How do I? Not on purpose.
Calm surprise, a flower unclosed.

   A fine flower,
one foot in the grave,
   stiff ankle, unsteady leg,
peering where to situate
   next step.

But the way I burst up
   from deeps, detach
a buried habitat,
   re-enter,

a yes-but-little-lower-than;
   pink squalling inflorescence;
a hatching half old cilia,
   half mutant April wings.

I read somewhere
   just waking up can kill you.

ON BEING WORLDLY

I'll buy that "collage blouse"
   as advertisied "prismatic with
faux coins and stones"
   and zigzags of lamé
to run my Visa out of sight.
   No, no. Excess is vulgar . . .
such makings in my attic.

Yes, him, with wheelchair and accordion
   and sheepish dog, faux leg,
I passed on my way home.
   And her, a can of corn and one real
onion, in faux mink.
   The checkers priced us, and I thought
mine rang my diamond up. . . .
   Rejected finery's the story of my attic.

But in this first box there's a fabric collage,
   a patchwork my child sewed at six,
wetting the tip inch of the thread,
   rolling the damp knot off her thumb
like one creating comets;
   these buttons, tacked on,
from my antiques box, two iridescents
   and a peacock eye, hers to learn with
or waste, at my largesse.

She must have worked their placement
   out with care. Or did she court
the throw of dice—much like
   the scraps they're sewn to,
and the years
   of new jobs, lovers, bits
of exultant paintings, sudden
   phone calls, and accrued birthdays—

a fading roulette I all by myself
   hold out, interrogate,
and fold back up, and hear
   as nowhere else in the whole house
the wind from the world terrestrial,
   sweeping the eaves and sparking
the spiderwebs.

DAYTIME MOON

Wax moon in a blue sky,
   do you hear night calling?
You hope to get there
   tomorrow? Thursday? Never?
Poor traveler, breathless, alone—
   no planet aunt, no bodyguard Mars.
Day-blinded, your night-eyes straining.
Take heart! The calendar is going to
   put carrots in your cheeks,
   and you'll unpack
   all your prescription stars.

Roses snag bricks, hook hats.
The caterer does not smile.
The hostess does not cook.
We, overdressed,
might layer down to Jefferson,
to Berkeley even,
jug shards of Jamestown.

Only alfresco.
Coifed boxwoods arch politely.
Birdhouse admits wrens only.
Tongues spin from antique tunes:
Rain lashing all DelMarVa   On
Portobello Road   I think
don't you one likes one's own things

A hiss—*Samantha!*
A porcelain on the lawn, holding
initialed fork, bird occupied.
Won't shoo.
His graceless neck jerks.
Bony bill, a bit, dissecting, jabs,
his wiry toes astride
the crusty wing.
Not one futilely fluttering ringed claw
can make him quit.

THE ACCIDENTAL PRISONER

Will anybody find me
under my own back porch?
I cut some sprigs of mint, then
ducked in here to check
the dryer vent. The door swung-to
and clicked. At one slam,
under everything, porch floor
and kitchen, 911, my empty house.
The neighbors in their shrubs
conjectural.
       A Bastille
daylight lattices this cell.

I think I left a burner on.
Could firemen hear me
above the basso
of their radios?
Will I get thirsty? Miss lunch?
One could relieve oneself,
there's privacy.
       A bunch
of stained, chipped flowerpots.
Clay saucers. Some unaccountable
bright straw. A bag of ossified
Sakrete to sit on,
if one could sit.
Trapped possums pace.

Come on. The door's just lattice.
One hinge is even loose.

My banging with a stone
bruises my thumbnail till it bleeds.
It hurts. *Loose* isn't *weak*.

Nobody comes. . . .
Prisioners do tunnel under. . . .

>Last summer we drove by our cemetery,
>admiring its retired antiquity,
>its roses shrouding bony trellises.
>so musical with texts and poetry,
>so in demand, the next
>lot's been annexed—a glaring
>scrub with stubblefield
>and one or two slick slabs. . . .

I could have washed these pots
and filled them with rosemary.

Nota bene, my survivors: I'm to be buried
in the old part of the cemetery.

DISSONANCE

tonight in Chopin's
    loved odd-legged dance
        pain tacit   hear
past-child's breath indrawn
    pale silent   near
        boxwoods   a stubblefield
past-mother
    clutching long hot switch
        struck
by his silence   pallor
    queer dry eyes (I'll
        never whip that
one again) she
    never did it only wanted
        his own child's words he
is not listening to Chopin or
    anything
        not to me

HOW HE RETURNED THANKS

Always the same one,
    sometimes so tired, his elbow on the table,
forehead propped on yawning palm,
    his eyes sealed as the dead.
The rest of us—upstairs or in the yard,
    delaying, finishing a something.
She
    might drop down on a chair an instant
then spring back stovewards,
    towel a long-tailed holder
for the hot bread pan.
    Sometimes all there we bowed in unison
with squinched-up ears.
    Still,
around his table. Beside him
    she
who'd cooked something good.
    Opening eyes we looked out through the window
to garden's twisted, sky-launched vines
    and yellow mandolins of squash,
and caught a rising flume,
    a string straight up and up
as bound to get somewhere.

THE FARMER IN THE DELL

Walking walking
   my gritty field beside the railroad track
      plow guttering the grass between corn rows
Sam shies at every vine, fat Jule slowpokes,
   lets him pull the plow—
      Flick her with the line!

         restraints . . . our only option now

Walking   hoofs high-stepping   corn
   blades nicking   grasshoppers
      whistling through their teeth   turn-
ing where corn stalks spindle,
   woods-roots grab out   swill
     rain that fell for corn

Plowing from woods to railroad track
   now back   walking   walking
    wind sweeps my face
sun fades my hat
   plow lines wrapped tight
     around my wrists

         Are these too tight, Nurse?

Our ten feet stepping
   muffled   our silent shoes
    the whispering of dirt to plow
Walking
   toward sundown,
    crop laying-by, and cash
Rounding the rows
   Clods rolling
    our ten feet stepping

The streak of clay
   that chalks this field
      was laid before it was my field
Before the hills in order stood
   or earth received her frame

          —can't have him getting up

My hell-hill field, rows
   winding, unraveling,
      a ball of binder-twine,
down to the meadow,
   noonday rising hot
      Kick out a rock
and fling it at the woods
   Rocks make good dirt   someday
      A woods-edge strung with rocks
Dirt terraces that break
   with three days' rain
      and wash away downhill

          Can't spare a nurse now just for him

Stop   shake out gravels
   tie my friendly shoe
      Look back across the fields   There stand
the windows and the yard
   She's crossing it
      taking the dry clothes in   alone
perched on that world
   with pump and washpot   her
      little arms and legs

          This should calm him. . . .

Walking to church the packed red road
　　we size up Clyde's crops on the way
　　　　It pays to fertilize　　She nods
My black shoes creak the bridge
　　to Uncle Fred's to take him cake
　　　　shout out about the wheat
who's sick who's dead who was at church
　　hear him repeat: "I used to could
　　　　Plowed many a day till after light . . . this
quilt is nearly　　look here
　　worn right through. . . ."

　　　　　　　　　—*make it through the night?*

These hills of mist of mine
　　these meadows of ground-fog
　　　　and morning glories
It's water holds them up　　pink
　　flars all water　　ditch
　　　　oozing　　emptying somewhere
My meadow field　　richest softest
　　blackest and pink flars
　　　　shrinking up　　they're done
black ditches　　walking　　walking
　　walking walking walking
　　　　walking

O LAMP

After tornado wrenched
our cabin out of line
my father rebuilt down the hill
a reeking bungalow, new pine,
three chimneys, and a high front porch.

My mother moved the lamps.
Now, walk behind me, babe.
Both in our coats. Down the dirt road,
glass font well up, firm hands around its waist,
its see-through, brass-clipped chimney tight,
its unlit wick looped dreamily in oil.

Winter sun. No flame. We walk.
She is ahead. I follow. I keep following.

There seems a light there,
seems some glint,
something blazed in print;
some shadow from her hands,
not from the sun.
This has gone on so long
the lamp's grown to her arm,
the arm is a relic,
the light's dropped back, it's
changed its residence.

THE DIARY

1

Too much like myself,
it listens critically.
Edits, though seldom rereads.
In the margins: *here incoherent.*

Like me, it mumbles.
The more I "Speak up, girl!"
the less it says outright,
wants in fact to not say.

2

Contrary to belief, the word *diary*
means undivulged; clues trail
the pages and the trail breaks off,
scent's lost. Wandering is
the only way out of this place.

Yet the helpless subjugation
to the daily task,
the need for trysting-place,
love for the white-hot page
that drains the wound, seals it.

3

I know the heroines of the craft—
the small-town wife, the *clear some,*
cloudy some fretful refrain
in her doubtful second marriage;
Jane Carlyle's war with crowing cocks.

To whom? To me. They write to me.
From pages hidden in the covered wagon,
"I said nothing, but I thought the more."
(But in a letter home:

"We are at the mercy of a madman.")
Missing, Fanny Kemble's account
of the night she fled upriver.

4
How to confide the footsteps of a shroud
under your window in the night?
The denials, the costumed felons
lurk in your wakings, nervously
pressing mustaches over their teeth.

Why are those scuds of gulls
hanging over the swamp today?

I, splashing, choking, struggling,
sinking in self-sight—

Oh, that little straw!

*

Cloud Cover

Today I want a silent poem.
Not one word dripping from a tree.
Trees, standing shadowless,
shadowless the spaces between.

Between sky and garden
shadows hesitate all day,
all day finger to the lips.
The eyes, unmoving, listen.

There is no air.
No clouds. One mist hangs
almost to the ground—word-
weary. Something lost
in the unshaded shadows?
Something firing from x distance
a mute torpedo?

JOE BOLTON, 1969–1990

Don't cry. You know
I wouldn't forget you.

I've known these—
    lads, for proper distance—
        known the charged body,
eyes prisming the mirror,
    the grinning kid, strutting
        into town behind his face,
stoning himself to absence,
    calling from light-fractured streets
        back to Kentucky twilight,
Rhonda, Jeffry, Star!
    you wouldn't leave me
        to face a life like this. . . .
Probing his destiny
    confused cameraman
        focused in the direction of the echo—
the head-on, the blast.
    Drinking, essentially alone, though she
        is/was in the kitchen,
and the Mexicans downstairs
    whoop up being out of jail

                Come. You must open the door
                to the room where you are,
                and look about for the mind's
                amalgam, the rueful pigtail
                you wanted to accentuate,
                the onesome before your mother
                ran away.
                        Driving home fast
                gray birds fell near the car
                like meteors, into the black
                water, into ink, gunmetal.

Who are/were you?
The little bit you tell me.
(But more than Rhonda knew.)

A grinning kid.
    I stand by helpless,
        as one watching an admired neighbor
taken away, but no right
    to go forward or to weep.
        The disturbing marvel,
dead when I got there,
    Chopin, Baudelaire,
        living in the dissonance
music calls harmony.

You'd slept with words.
How could you abort the issue
now? Abort fate? Whether the fate
was yours or its, you couldn't tell
for sure, but it was sure.

He's grief.
    He comforts grief.
        Knew what's sustenance.
Not scraps of table talk, but pages'
    storehouse, their storehouses,
        the wriggling words
that leap from sun to sun
    and feed the solitary multitude,
        the solitary one.

Don't cry.
I wouldn't forget you.

Find Me

by my trail of fragments,

                    stale crumbs,

      green broken boughs
      of protocol.
       Footprints
all missteps,

    tatters of sackcloth
     on the undergrowth,

confused backtracks.
      A rough HELP
lipsticked on a map
  tossed out too far
       with backbite cream.
                 Here
left the highway

    for the woods
pressed jungleward.   Discover

   a trace of desiccated residue
       staining a sheet of paper

struggling to speak.

THESE GIFTS

Fred Ross, 1913–1993

We take nothing out of this world

except yarns you invented at
   the feedsack that fed the planter
   as it worked the pear-tree field
   minding small sibling in straw hat,
except the willow at the springhead
   you dug out (home for the funeral I saw only
   workers pouring out of Textiles-Cone),
the non-curricular you majored
   in   your rabbit boxes   bantam
   Easter egg that outpipped
   all your cousins',
your silly melon crop that   green-
   streaked hogs   wallowed branchside
   your gun where is it? and the squirrels
   you toppled out of trees and ate fried,
your diary's secrets (rouged schoolgirls
   trailed me down the playground:
   "Tell Fra-yd—I love him!"),
   the banjo that you swapped a jacket
   for then yo-lee-lay-hooed to
   on front steps at dusk,

the empties clinking in your desk
   among the last abandoned novel's
   pages (music that knows that winning loses),
except your grim voice miles away
   after my *You spend your day*—?:
   Waiting for dark!
even last year's tall skeletal
   smile that took me by the hand
   never a *Mayday mayday* from the stark

porch's canes and
                calendars wherein
our parents called down
to the last one up *Be sure*
to put the fire to bed;

you take your cache that flares and flashes
    out   a recent breath.

LAST ANT

They scutter in my dreams, the ants
that left the flower pot,
        that third plant
        I watched die, one of three
basils rescued from the freeze.
A fungus or mildew.
        I had to pull it up
        and leave the soil to dry.

Then ants began to come out,
cross the crater, the dusty
        desert of old potting soil;
        every appendage twitching, they explored
the great clay wall,
the width of plastic saucer,
        white longitude of sill,
mad for a jot to drink.
The natural thing to do was kill them all.

This morning, one more ant
ran wildly—he knew where?—
a straight line toward the sink.

Someone at the University
might take his questions:
        why there's no rainfall
        anymore, what happened to his
habitat, how Edens dry
up suddenly—in short, why
        he's endangered—things
        in his compound eyes not simple.

I gave the coup de grâce,
a little overkill (his bony suit)
        before I took the pot outside,
        and washed my hands.

AUGUST DOVES

Haze
The garden stops to catch
its breath   a swallow-

    tail's reconnaissance   a
    sense of Canada   Alaska

too   the North Pole   but
the doves have brought a young
one to the flower bed
sliding trompe l'oeil among

the columbines come out
at iris   new one
flings wings across a stepping-stone

    panning damp edges'
    flicking-gold-tipped grubs
    a banner in sun-
    shine   a vernal sheen   won't

take a hint   the two   keep
noiselessly cross-sweeping

    not a word   their nest-
    frayed wings glint rusty
    rounds to high first-loosening leaves

WHY ANGELS CHOIR

Solitude cries out
    and makes no noise.
I need a cat to talk to.
    A dog's more on the spot.

Talk to yourself—the TV.

Phone, ring.
    French, German, Hindi—
It's the tongue.
    Has needs.

Some language
    programs certain cells
will long unseen old
    farms and half-lit rooms, brief
smiles, chores. What's sane.

It's why birds sing. For hours
    arranged on branches
touching panes,
    none listening
to another. Nobody's listening
    to anybody else.

Out on a sunny wire
    one mockingbird
says things severe,
   makes lists, gets it all
off his chest.

In this house, silence, heavy.

A little lower that the Aves.

CUTS BUTTONS OFF AN OLD SWEATER

It takes a needle to complete the job—
    pick the two choked eyes empty of the thread,
    pick out the particles of sweater wool.
It takes a dark, thin book to tray the pickings
    (they're hard to gather off her skirt, the floor)
    and chute them in the trash can;
    takes her tea-tin container for
    such buttons, flat, dime-sized,
    that might be useful on another sweater,
    a weary blouse, some baby shirt.
It takes good light, the three-way study lamp,
    though by the window, and midafternoon.
And it takes time. Minutes she crooked from the hour,
    shoplifted from the day,
    head bent to these useful buttons,
    to this devised delay.

This is no dream. Real light, real time, real fingers.

The dream was
    elbowing,
    with flying arms,
    slack, lazy bloom;
    wading armed goldenrod
    splashing around the shoulders;
    crashing tall ironweed,
    hushed, purple fireworks
    whispering fragrance
    and light years of taking leave,
    leave-taking exuberant, with blowing hair,
    and sun, sunlight, light of sun stars comets.
That is, an hour of some real use,
    and never mind old sweaters and
    good buttons undone underfoot.

WORLDS OLD AND NEW:
FATHER LOPEZ, LA FLORIDA, 1565–1569

For Mike Gannon

A two-inch name deep in two hundred pages,
   his span strewn over eight: Fleet Chaplain with
Menendez out of Cádiz sailing for Florida.

Stooped, prematurely bald, a theologue
   too drab to venerate? Or beautiful,
a graceful *angelo* to captivate
   a graceless people and no need enshrine in books?
Perhaps robust, a cassocked soldier prized
   for brawn more than for words.

Himself undocumented, he made note
   mid-voyage: a killer hurricane no one
predicted, the weary fleet struck head-on.
   The sea rose to the very clouds. I passed
the night confessing my companions.
   Three days, blind roar and frigid weight beat
merciless. *We drown. . . . Not yet . . .* The captain
   flinging casks out to the storm, *Take all, Sea Demons!*

When Jesus Christ permitted the return
   of day we looked at one another
as men raised from the dead.

Survived, the Puerto Ricans urged: Stay here.
   I asked Jesu to grant a greater charge—
His mission in the wilderness.

August 27: *Entering*
   Bahama Channel . . . about nine, evening . . .
a holy miracle. . . . A comet lit
   the sky, so bright it might have been the sun.

It floated toward the west, toward Florida,
    its brightness long enough for two Credos—
for half a minute, if run through in haste. . . .

and faded like the Spanish missions,
    soldiers and settlers gnawing ruddy bones,
starved horses' carcasses, their leather harness,
    cut down by fever, flux, and frost;
one longed for Fra Angelica's stark cell.

But on Mantanzas' bank Fray Lopez watched
    St. Augustine's entrenchments rise, saw come
ashore Menendez on the bannered path,
    trumpets and guns. *I took a Cross and went*
to him, singing Te Deum Laudamus. . . .
    He knelt and kissed the Cross, and so did all.
In this sublimity he noted
    Indians pantomiming, crossing, kneeling.

Just two years more, this Vicar of La Florida
    writing, inside coquina gates, to Spain,
hinted indisposition. 1567.
    The record stops. Whether he
saw Cádiz again, or lies near Marcos
    in sound of hum of motors, hiss of
drawbridge opening the Bridge of Lions
    for my motorboat, whether, unlike our
minister, who fell golfstick midair—
    he languished too dispirited to write—
nobody made a note of.

Nobody guessed I would be anxious
    four centuries on. Maybe—or not—they mourned
the ringing Te Deum Laudamus voice,
    but no one thought I would be fingering

these offset pages, thready letters—
    a place I hungered and explored, where he
knew nothing of predicted hurricanes,
    called meteors comets, faced unknown frontiers,
believed in resurrection of the flesh—
    and, coming on this blackout, feel a pang.

LATE DINNER

I knew you were expecting me
        but—was held up.
Thing couldn't wait,
        popsicles melting and the freezer far;
had clothes to bring in from the rain.
        I ran, but they were always damp;
and diapers to be changed, pail full;
        something burning somewhere,
something indefinable, and self-contained,
        one hoped. But I
avoided confrontation with that long
        scorch in pink orchard flesh.
On top of everything
        I took a wrong turn,
a street I hadn't known about,
        nobody'd told me.
In those days maps were bad.

        But here I am.
Brandy and shortbread?
        That will do.

SHAKING THE PLUM TREE

Such light there was.
Ben up the plum tree,
   red plums snaked with light,
gold veins jagging in the plum skins
   like metal boiling,
plums bolting, knocking, to the ground,
   the sky, a huge shade-tree of light
tenting the stubblefield with centigrade,
   the pine woods' lashes, glass,
the girls' frocks, pale with glare,
   the voile geraniums, fading,
only the sheer hats shading
   the jelly cheeks dark red
and the simmering eyes,
   coming to a boil.

ALWAYS RECLUSIVE,

I'm constructing my own brierpatch. True,
I'm still bleeding from the first canes I dug in;
thorns fight off cultivation, cut both ways;
they like barbwiring things in
as much as battling guests; that's useful;
I won't try getting out too soon, say for a
tipsy fruit, or reckless stroll. What I don't spend
on tickets I'll apply on long long-distance calls.

Hunters will come and shake my fence, dogs panting,
paws pointing. I'll like that. I'll cuddle up
and turn the page.

"The blackberry, permitted its own way,
is an unmanageable plant." Here's a
variety called *Taylor*: "Season late,
bush vigorous, hardy . . . free from rust."
That's it. Don't let my brierpatch rust.

A HAREM OF HENS

They flock to him,
   his brilliant aging students,
     old friends' widows,
       friends' divorced wives.
Now he no longer teaches,
   lectures, or signs autographs,
     his one companion Uncommitted Cat
     (not blooded by felicitously
marked and furred), he grows
   exotic lettuces, sweet carrots and
     lipped orchids, voluptuous
       goldfish covert in a leafy pond,
and ornamental hens in wire condos.

He gives a learned devotee
   a tour of nests:
        his Koreanna,
   lacquered onyx, gold and copper;
     Polischa, turbaned, in long pants;
and Geisha, a damasked long-legs, powder blue.

She marshals critical acumen to construe.

Their eyes, exclusive,
         pop her
   jealous shots. Mamselle, black feather
     collar splaying her white breast,
       sits-nest stiff as a paperweight,
by turns turns on Glad Eager Scholar
   a mad stare and a sleepy scowl.
     He smiles. "De-termined
       to lay an egg all by herself."

LIKE ONE CONCUSSED

Like one concussed, he wakes.
Where's this?
A hole's bombed in the barracks.
He knows damnwell
there is no window there.
This quiet should not be.
He sweats. The tanks have
left without me, one lost survivor.
                    His hot cheek
grazes lace and lofted down;
the blue wall's whispering.
Bare feet, deep mirror's face,
his, his, his. Oh I do
thee wed, this place.

CONTEMPLATING JAILBREAK

Through the bars?
   surrender
   saw my music?
   scissors my embroidery?
I was making masks for a rabbit
      using the bag the river came in
            a few holes

marriage was an economy all round

how I got here   halt   four corners
halt again   that's another story

the judge would not lean down
   but my testimony is
                  he swore
I'll come throw the moon
   over your shoulder every night
pay me when you can

after that nights were scarce
   when's frequent
halt   doing time

however
      finally
   I didn't want September
days longer   a length of chiffon
   slithering over drab pines
         just what I can't use

somehow too had fallen in love
   with that mink sitting above
December on some snow
   a treatise: save your skin

however
   some coats   designated goods
the spot lit
   hit me

I thought how well it was arranged
   the magic carpet bedside
the turbaned engineer
                     Get on—
a dream to take us miles away
the letter-flap was folded back
   I sealed the pillow

my testimony is
   in the beginning
my bed had
little round china rolling feet
that's why

ENDING WINTER

My letter's sleeping somewhere
   on the way to,
his address and mine (smaller)
   briefly shared.
I stand at my window
   biting a hard pear.
After a fruitless winter
   my ego is leafing
but won't bloom this year.

Night Retrieves

Smoking forest and red bees
snapped-off at zenith
    don't care for
        morning, nor
my yard's plaited trees.

I was looking for holly? With Benedict?
He'd just called back,
"Here's some!" I, hurrying to
the sought-for ache.

Gone.
    All
hung by a silk to
wide waste, a There
no echoes, no tints refracted,
streets of St. Augustine
laid in Gambier, time-quaked.

Woods, voice retract.
A gray arachnid
that sleeps all day
and sews up the night,
spinneret ingathering with care,
primordial eyes shut tight,
never loses a stitch
of my long laddered snare.

    Where, Benedict?

SITTING IN THE DARK, MORNING

No chink anywhere.

Edges of gray
    gouache a square:

My big pane
    made for light.

Entangled shapes, black trees,
    brightening, declassify:
        maple, pine, green
        of black cherry.

No. Clods, ruins of my box,
    ascending through stained clay
        to grass, green
        swells of graves.

No. Square of backyard
    from my room's refuge,
        dodging friendly fire,
        coward.

Farther:
    prospect of countryside,
        square night, horizon-lit
        from long high porch; petunias,
        world laid out wide.

Halo in dark.

CONVERSE

I'm a woman at a window
talking to a man outside.
                    My elbow's
on the sill. The carved
        acanthus leaves
        behind me wheeze
with dust.
        Some other leaves
crush
        underneath his shoes
        flat on the canvas
(you can't hear this of course).

The artist has two guises
in one time
and so must I.

Pretend a 16-wheeler
                        booms
past just out of frame,
rattling long emptiness
on our moot commune.
Then say I know this man:
(I, she) Where the dust of the day
        meets the dust of the night.
(He) Don't be decadent.
(I, she) Right.

In the room behind me, in
the real house I stand in,
a voice rises and falls
                    in paints,
separates in parts:
                    somebody—
it's that man

pitched back to life,
                    I can
tell by his eyes
(which you'll never see—
                    they're shaded
in, averted, as if autistic,
                    and they're dead).
But he's still playing
rending variations on a tune
after cicadas,
a summer's ending,
                    the summer's ending,
that summer's ending.

I take it up, humming,
or have taken it up.

He stands before me. But I
don't listen. Why
am I humming?
                    I'm humming.

And
never having heard
my voice from a distance
I turn my ear
                    softly
back into the picture

acritically. Do I like
        what I hear?
Shall I hum? Or sing
        out clear?

CAT

That gray cat scouts my creek
at twilight, infiltrating
and assembling night.
I think new people have moved in
next door where that old lady died,
but he still hides among agaves.

> I keep an eye on him as I set in
> the burglar bars here
> at my last-ditch creek—
> mud cave-in, floating
> burger wrappers, cups.

I lose him as night falls.
His prowl? His past? His kin? His kill?

> Painkiller and flashlight in reach,
> I drowse.

Dog's solo howl.
Drunk at gunpoint? An idle meteor?
The foreseen hour?

> Locked up. Alarm set. The usual
> gray paws rattling my door.

ONE LAST WARM DAY

One last warm day
on the devised chair
on the devised floor,
aura of tree,
its canned sun spewing
mixed-spectrum stars.

Bugs work the paving.
One probes our aging
Homo sapiens foot,
courting a big bang,
won't stop:
hunts murky matter
where nothing starts,
where what's beyond,
where that beyond ends.

Hordes
     purple   ocher   garnet
pulse small.

Last warm day.
Snug bone-carved chair.
Smooth marbled stones
bear feet. Green galaxies,
no twins, expand.

DEER

Six long-time friends Scotch—
    drinking dusk to night.
        Two fawns, it seems—
        hard to make out—
        male and female,
        shrub by shrub
over long grounds, halt in plain sight.

Can he see in?
    Those running leaps.
        At us?
        Wan boozers
        in soft chairs?
He paws and leaps and nears. She grazes on.

Our small fire's out,
    canes on the floor.
        We rise.
        This something
        targeting our dusk,
        our auld lang glass?
        This something knows
something it has to do—
shatter a wall and jump through.

AFTON MOUNTAIN

Once, coming over Afton Mountain
    my husband bent on
        passing a slow truck,
the threesome gaze of passengers
    toward Ragged Mountain
        over valleys
jabbed
    by signposts   a house   a horse—
John Kirby-Smith exclaimed,
            "God! I wish
James Waller were alive
    and was here
        right this minute!" so forcibly
James Waller's laugh,
obese hand slapping obese thigh,
and reckless high-speed cracks,
cashed death in for a minute—a minute
    I relive recurrently,
        with less success progressively.
They say the Afton road is wider now,
    but I don't drive
        and as you know John Kirby-Smith is not alive.

HOMECOMING

Was it the tree or the wind
    that said something,
        a clatter of leaves and water
            as the gate shut,
a rush of explanations?
    The walk listened flatly,
        hardening its heart;
            at the front door
deadlock stiffed the key,
    no shower of words,
        and the tree, leaves
            flung dry, stared off
toward the airport.

Blessed are the brave,
      for their skulls shall be crushed
Blessed are the merciful,
      they shall be tortured
Blessed are the idealistic,
      they shall despair
Blessed are the generous,
      their bones shall be picked clean
Blessed are the achievers,
      they shall exchange achievement for life
Blessed are the accepting,
      they shall be buried under a mausoleum of woe

COCOON

He's in intensive care, a coma,
the neighbor I lunched with last month,
astonished, still, his house
so nondescript outside
was lined with years of
vintage craved by Christie's:
with prints and serried maps
in frames he made himself
(hours of mitered molding
and distressed hand-rubbing);

woodwork he made himself,
his delicate long hands
guiding the saw, tacking
the molding into panels
to dress up doors, making old
mantels to match one really old;
folding, above the salvaged lead-glass
window lugged from England,
a red silk valance shot and
fringed with gold, flickering
out tarnished earls and witches;

painted kings and Buddhas
staring from four walls,
pop-eyed stitches in past time
weirdly transported, transmitted,
transmogrified, implanted in his house,
his nest, his chrysalis, his semidormant,
nightclothes, saw-toothed dream.

Yes, I expect any hour now.

CLOTHES FROM THREE PLANETS

May

Winter climbs the attic
    to safe mothballs   shimmer
      flutters down   summer
mountains   December tropics

1
These T-shirts strode the Avenida
    watched   far out great gunning waves
      set for a long campaign

Absurd embroidered arms crave
    still   *castillos* and drawbridges
      the blood of their bloodstains

2
In this space summer gear   tired
    shreds of parachutes and fearful
      falling moons   raiment of chancels
rising out of steeps that well
    from valley floors   Sewanee fogs   distance
      relaying to infinity

3
Home planet runs its yearly track
    on treadmill attic steps
      The old caged squirrel   *elle s'amuse*

It's work

KITCHEN FABLE

The fork lived with the knife
    and found it hard—for years
took nicks and scratches,
    not to mention cuts.

She who took tedium by the ears:
    nonforthcoming pickles,
defiant stretched-out lettuce,
    sauce-gooed particles.

He who came down whack.
His conversation, even, edged.

Lying beside him in the drawer
    she formed a crazed patina.
The seasons stacked—
    melons, succeeded by cured pork.

He dulled; he was a dull knife,
while she was, after all, a fork.

THE HOSTAGE

They think of me, in their health.

No corridors where shoes whisper.

> (Once I was seven, my tonsils
> somewhere else in the hospital.)

In their dark,
until the blanket gets warm
they think of me.

Sometimes I'm in their dream:
the happy, ravaged fantasy,
without blood and flesh,   no

> whether it's going to hurt,
> how long it's going to hurt,
> how long it's going to hurt that much.

They write cards
at the commercials. Between
to and fro.
Answerlessness is a fence
in a film war.

They think of me
not in Latin or Arabic:
in the alphabet they know.

They speak of me,
begging recollection,
then sweating out chimera:
my blue eyes, my step, my grin.

They will never beg to see my scar.

THE SKY-WATCHER

Prowlers
   have scared the stars away.
She sets
   her outside light for six;
her neighbor
   burns his all night every night.
The city
   sends a van with a lift-basket
and a man
   to change street bulbs by schedule.

Some mornings,
   in the so-called dark, she gives up
searching
   Venus between chimneys and
massed leaves,
   turns out the lamps, and sits
with all
   the shades up in the living room.
Vast frames
   of light hang on the walls.
Umbrella
   and cane handles rise, gibbous,
in expanses
   unexplained. She watches the
fluorescent rays
   from kitchen louvers crosshatch
bookshelves,
   emitting black dimensions, stygian
and pure.
   A chair projects a symbol,
malformed,
   on the floor, and Berenice's Hair,
blowing
   somewhere, showers her human arm.

LIFT-OFF

She made her first flight
just short of ninety.
Never afraid, might have
at any time, and always
said, though our car stood
on jacks in 1932 (no time
to treat for lessons), "I could.
I know I could have driven."

She walked the mile to church;
then rode with neighbors. Sometimes
a cousin took her for a drive.
On Saturdays watched keenly,
from the front porch, "people pass."

Later traveling prone cross-state
in the back seat of our car,
remote and ill, she roused:
"Are those—mountains? . . .
Beautiful."

It would have been exuberance
to fly back with her,
look down on rambling
cars and rivers (*Beautiful*).

However, we ourselves drove down
and met her coffin at the funeral home.
She got there first.

LATE LEISURE

Some things achieve finale;
vivace to larghetto;
three hundred pages, *End*;
threescore and ten, of course,
    that's it.

But this embroidery that I
inch aimlessly along
could be found years from now
wadded unfinished
    in a basket.

I, past my expiration date,
fold the cloth twice for center,
my needle threaded for the first
small stitch, myself
    capriciously ongoing.

I see it, as a sampler, challenging.
It has a long, protracted feel—
the dog each morning barking at the gate,
just where I left him
    yesterday.

I'll flesh out by the millimeter
a gawky shepherdess,
a time-lapse Federal house beyond,
odd birds and fish to signify
    earth floundering on,

the alphabet that's used
for English, French, Italian—
more tongues that I will speak
in this life, but fewer than birdcalls
    I recognize.

I'll work through color changes
almost photosynthetic;
I'll search out chairs by windows
in south-facing rooms;
     I'll never work by artificial light.

The sun won't cast a shadow of these men.
The curly beasts submit to cubist life
as in some static dream
the dead dream in their sleep,
     some plastic intervention.

If I get to the last rows
of this kit, I'll have to find
another one as slow and interim;
     but no need plan that yet.